FRANZ LISZT

TOTENTANZ
DANSE MACABRE

Paraphrase über „Dies irae"

FÜR KLAVIER – FOR PIANO SOLO

Herausgegeben von – Edited by

Imre SULYOK
Imre MEZŐ

Vorwort von – Preface by

Adrienne KACZMARCZYK

NEUE, ERWEITERTE AUSGABE
NEW, ENLARGED EDITION

EDITIO MUSICA BUDAPEST

Editio Musica Budapest Zeneműkiadó Kft.
1132 Budapest, Visegrádi utca 13. • Tel.: +36 1 236-1104
E-mail: emb@emb.hu • Internet: www.emb.hu

ABKÜRZUNGEN – ABBREVIATIONS

BL-B = *Briefwechsel zwischen Franz Liszt und Hans von Bülow*, hg. von La Mara (Leipzig: Breitkopf & Härtel, 1898) — **Br.** = *Franz Liszts Briefe*, Bd. I–VIII, hg. von La Mara (Leipzig: Breitkopf & Härtel, 1893–1905) — **D-WRgs** = Klassik Stiftung Weimar, Goethe- und Schiller-Archiv — **ELL** = *Liszt Ferenc válogatott levelei (1824–1861)*, válogatta, fordította és jegyzetekkel ellátta Eckhardt Mária [*Ferenc Liszt, Selected Correspondence (1824–1861)*, ed. by Mária Eckhardt] (Budapest: Zeneműkiadó, 1989) — **H-Bl** = Budapest, Liszt Ferenc Zeneművészeti Egyetem, Liszt Ferenc Emlékmúzeum és Kutatóközpont [The Liszt Ferenc Academy of Music, Liszt Ferenc Memorial Museum and Research Centre] — **HM** = *Musikalisch-literarischer Monatsbericht neuer Musikalien, musikalischer Schriften und Abbildungen* (Leipzig: Hofmeister,1829–1947) — **K-LLT** = Adrienne Kaczmarczyk: „Liszt, Lamennais und der *Totentanz*", *Studia Musicologica* 43/1–2 (2002), S. 53–72 — **Md'A-M** = *Mémoires, souvenirs et journaux de la Comtesse d'Agoult (Daniel Stern)*, tomes I–II, présentation et notes de Charles F. Dupêchez (Paris: Mercure de France, 1990) — **MLTS** = Rena Charnin Mueller: *Liszt's 'Tasso' Sketchbook: Studies in Sources and Revisions*, Ph. D. Diss. (New York University, 1986) — **NG2** = *The New Grove Dictionary of Music and Musicians*, 2nd edition, ed. by Stanley Sadie (London: Macmillan Publishers, 2001) — **NG2** plus a number = numbering in Mária Eckhardt–Rena Charnin Mueller, 'Franz Liszt, Works', in NG2, vol. 14, pp. 785–872 — **NLA** = Franz Liszt: *Neue Ausgabe sämtlicher Werke* (Budapest: Editio Musica Budapest, 1970–) — **NLE** = Ferenc Liszt: *New Edition of the Complete Works* (Budapest: Editio Musica Budapest, 1970–) — **PFL** = Richard Pohl: *Franz Liszt. Studien und Erinnerungen* (Leipzig: B. Schlick, 1883) — **R** = Dr. Felix Raabe: „Verzeichnis aller Werke Liszts nach Gruppen geordnet", in Peter Raabe: *Franz Liszt*, Bd. II: Liszts Schaffen, 2., ergänzte Ausgabe (Tutzing: Schneider, 1968), 241–377, Zusätze 7–40 — **RLKM** = Lina Ramann: *Franz Liszt. Als Künstler und Mensch*, Bd. I, II/1, II/2 (Leipzig: Breitkopf & Härtel, 1880, 1887, 1894) — **SH** = Michael Short–Leslie Howard: 'F. Liszt: List of Works', comprehensively expanded from the Catalogue of Humphrey Searle as revised by Sharon Winklhofer, in *Quaderni dell'Istituto Liszt* 3 (Milano: Rugginenti, 2004) — **SW** = Humphrey Searle, rev. by Sharon Winklhofer: 'Franz Liszt, Works', in *The New Grove Early Romantic Masters*, vol. 1: *Chopin, Schumann, Liszt* (New York & London: Macmillan, 1985) — **US-NYpm** = New York, The Pierpont Morgan Library — **US-Wc** = Washington, DC, The Library of Congress

INHALT – CONTENTS

ZUR AUSGABE

Die Veröffentlichung der Kompositionen, Schriften und der Korrespondenz von Franz Liszt (1811–1886) sowie die Einordnung seines schöpferischen Lebenswerkes im Rahmen eines Katalogs begann im 20. Jahrhundert und dauert auch heute noch an. Die Veröffentlichung der Gesamtausgabe des musikalischen Lebenswerkes eröffnete die von Großherzog Carl Alexander von Sachsen-Weimar-Eisenach gegründete und durch die Herzogin Marie von Hohenlohe unterstützte Franz Liszt-Stiftung im Jahre 1907. Hierbei handelt es sich um die so genannte alte Gesamtausgabe, deren bis 1936 entstandenen 33 Bände ein Drittel des Lebenswerkes beinhalten. Die Modernisierung und die Beendigung dieser Publikation sich zum Ziele setzend initiierte die Editio Musica Budapest (EMB) im Jahre 1970 eine wissenschaftlich fundierte, neue, kritische Ausgabe des musikalischen Lebenswerkes.

Die Neue Liszt-Ausgabe (NLA) ist nach Gattung und Besetzung in zehn Serien unterteilt. Serie I (Werke für Klavier zu zwei Händen) lag in einer gemeinsamen Ausgabe von EMB und Bärenreiter-Verlag, Kassel, bis 1985 vor. Ab 1986 setzte EMB die Herausgabe der NLA eigenständig fort, und vollendete Serie II (Freie Bearbeitungen und Transkriptionen für Klavier zu zwei Händen) bis 2005. Das Grundprinzip der Edition der Serien I und II bestand darin, in erster Linie die endgültigen Fassungen der Werke zu veröffentlichen; von Frühfassungen erschienen im Anhang nur jene, die von der endgültigen Fassung wesentlich abweichen. 2005 begann die Herausgabe einer Reihe von 15 Supplementbänden mit dem Ziel, Frühfassungen der Werke für Klavier zu zwei Händen zu veröffentlichen, die von der endgültigen Fassung in geringerem Maße abweichen. In erster Linie sind es jene, die von Liszt selbst publiziert wurden, aber auch solche, die in Manuskript geblieben sind. In Spezialfällen werden auch umfangreichere Fragmente in den Supplementbänden publiziert.

Die Einzelausgaben der Klavierwerke Liszts, die in der NLA schon publiziert wurden, bieten nicht nur authentische, wissenschaftlich fundierte Notentexte samt kritischen Berichten, sondern auch komplette Frühfassungen und informative Vorwörter, die die Entstehungsgeschichte der jeweiligen Werke darstellt.

*

Wir waren bei der Edition bestrebt, die Besonderheiten der Kompositions- und Notationsweise Liszts weitestgehend zu berücksichtigen. Dementsprechend werden die irregulären, vereinfacht notierten Abschnitte nur dann den Regeln der heutigen Notation entsprechend umgestaltet, wenn dadurch das Notenbild nicht unnötig belastet wird. Der Rhythmus wurde nicht in regelmäßige Form gebracht, wo der Zeitpunkt des Anschlags eines Tones ausschließlich durch die Stellung dieses Tones bestimmt ist. Die Inkonsequenzen bei den Vereinfachungen werden dagegen in jedem Fall behoben. Die so genannte orchestermäßige Schreibweise ist überall beibehalten; die Notenstiele werden an solchen Stellen nicht in die übliche Richtung gezogen. Pausenzeichen bei zwei oder mehreren Stimmen in der gleichen Hand werden nur dann nachträglich gesetzt, wenn das Fehlen des Zeichens den Einsatz und die rhythmische Position der darauf folgenden Note unsicher gemacht hätte. Die Größe der Notenköpfe – normal (groß), kleiner und sehr klein – folgt genau den Quellen. Die aus einer Note bestehenden Vorschläge verschiedener Werte sind einheitlich als Achtel mit durchgestrichenem Stiel geschrieben; ihre Legatobögen wurden stillschweigend ergänzt. Der Wert der kleineren Noten wird nur dann korrigiert, wenn diese einen wesentlichen Bestandteil des Rhythmus bilden. Den Mehrwert der einen Hand und die ersetzenden Fermaten der anderen Hand, die über dem leeren Liniensystem stehen, werden unverändert belassen, Pausenzeichen wurden von uns unter ihnen nicht ergänzt. Bei chromatischen Bewegungen werden die Versetzungszeichen innerhalb des gleichen Taktes der besseren Lesbarkeit wegen mehrmals ausgeschrieben. Bei *quasi cadenza, a capriccio, a piacere* und *rubato* werden weder die Werte berichtigt, noch werden eventuelle Taktwechsel angemerkt. Die mit ossia überschriebenen, für Klaviere mit kleinerem Tonumfang als sieben Oktaven komponierten Abschnitte sind nur in den „Critical Notes" mitgeteilt, da sie für die heutige Praxis nicht mehr von Belang sind. Die ursprüngliche Bogensetzung der Quellen wird beibehalten und die gleichzeitig für zwei Stimmen geltenden Legatobögen bleiben ebenfalls unverändert. Wo die Quellen keinen Pedalgebrauch verlangen, wird er in dieser Ausgabe auch nicht vorgeschlagen, da das Fehlen der Bezeichnungen der Pedalführung nicht mit *senza pedale* identisch ist: die Anweisung *armonioso* verlangt z. B. einen ausgesprochen häufigen Gebrauch des Pedals. Beim Ausschreiben der Aufhebung von *una corda* wurde nicht nur die Dynamik, sondern auch der Tonfarbenwechsel berücksichtigt. Die *due pedali (mettez les deux pédales)* Anweisung der Quellen wird durch *con ped., una corda* ersetzt und die Veränderung jedes Mal in den „Critical Notes" erwähnt. Die in der Mitte zwischen den zwei Systemen stehenden >-Zeichen werden in beiden Händen ausgeschrieben. Die gestrichelte Linie nach Tempobezeichnungen wie *riten., accel.,* usw. zeigt die Geltungsdauer der gegebenen Anweisung an; folglich ist am Ende der gestrichelten Linie *a tempo* nicht extra ausgeschrieben. In den Werken ist Liszts ursprünglicher Fingersatz überall angegeben. Er wird nur in Fällen ergänzt, wo die Quellen den Fingersatz bei identischen Musikabschnitten erst an einer späteren Stelle oder Stellen mitteilen. Liszts eigenartige, heutzutage ungebräuchliche Vortragszeichen werden beibehalten. Von diesen beziehen sich die großen ∧, und > (Akzent-) sowie die ⌢ (Fermaten-) Zeichen auf die von ihnen umfasste Notengruppe. Die Bedeutung der anderen Zeichen wird in den Fußnoten zum Fall erklärt. *NB* bezeichnet immer eine Fußnote oder Anweisung, die der Vorlage entnommen ist, wogegen die mit Sternchen bezeichneten Fußnoten von den Herausgebern stammen. Ausnahmsweise kann auch eine mit einem Sternchen versehene Fußnote aus dem Original stammen; auf diesen Umstand weist dann die Bemerkung „Originalfußnote" hin.

Die Ergänzungen der Herausgeber werden folgendermaßen gekennzeichnet:

Buchstaben (Wörter, dynamische Bezeichnungen und *tr*-Zeichen) durch Kursivschrift;

Triolen- und andere Zahlen durch eine kleinere Schriftgröße und durch Kursivierung;

Versetzungszeichen, Staccatopunkte und -keile, Pedalzeichen, Pedalsternchen, Tenuto- und Akzentzeichen, Fermaten und Ornamente durch einen sehr feinen kleineren Stich;

Crescendo- und Diminuendo-Zeichen, runde Klammern, Triller-Wellenlinien, große Akzentzeichen und Fermaten durch dünne Linien;

Taktvorzeichen durch dünn gedruckte Zahlen zwischen den zwei Systemen;

Bögen durch Strichelung;

Taktstriche durch Punktierung.

Alle anderen Ergänzungen stehen in eckigen Klammern.

Um den praktischen Zielsetzungen der NLA zu entsprechen und bei der Lösung von Problemen des Vortrages der Werkes zu helfen, haben die Herausgeber auch Liszts mündliche Vortragsanweisungen mit aufgenommen, die August Göllerich über Liszts Klavierstudien in seinem Tagebuch aufzeichnete und die in Lina Ramanns *Liszt-Pädagogium* sowie in anderen zuverlässigen Aufzeichnungen erhalten geblieben sind.

Zur Erleichterung der Identifizierung der Werke ist auch ihre Nummer im Werkverzeichnis von Raabe, Searle–Winklhofer, Eckhardt–Mueller und Short–Howard angegeben.

VORWORT

TOTENTANZ – DANSE MACABRE
Paraphrase über „Dies irae"
R 188, SW/SH 525, NG2 A62

Der *Totentanz / Danse macabre* ist eines der wichtigsten Ergebnisse der Weimarer Schaffenszeit, obwohl die Entstehungsgeschichte des Werks die Grenzen dieses Zeitraums in beiden Richtungen überschreitet. Den inspirierenden Hintergrund bilden jene musikalischen und künstlerischen Ereignisse, deren Teil Liszt in den 1830er Jahren war; die Veröffentlichung erfolgte jedoch erst 1865, nachdem Liszt schon nach Rom umgezogen war.

Die Absicht, die der Komposition zugrunde liegende „Dies irae"-Melodie zu verarbeiten, beschäftigte Liszt vermutlich bereits seit Dezember 1830, seit der Pariser Uraufführung von Berlioz' *Symphonie fantastique*. Sein frühes Interesse belegen die bis 1833 mit außergewöhnlicher Sorgfalt angefertigte Klavierpartitur der Sinfonie[1] sowie die Tatsache, dass er für den *Totentanz* eine die Alternatim-Praxis repräsentierende Bearbeitung der Sequenz französischer Herkunft zur Grundlage gewählt hatte.[2] Darin wurden die ungeraden Strophen zu der Thomas von Celano zugeschriebenen originalen Melodie gesungen, die geraden zu einem vierstimmigen Musikmaterial aus der Neuzeit, das bei Liszt in der 6. Variation (Takt 466) erscheint.[3]

Der konkrete Kompositionsplan kann zunächst mit einem Tagebucheintrag vom Februar 1839 in Zusammenhang gebracht werden. Liszt trug zwei in Gattung und Besetzung nicht näher bestimmbare Werktitel ins Tagebuch ein, der eine ist mit dem Namen Holbein, der andere mit dem Orcagnas verbunden.[4] Den mit dem Namen des deutschen Malers assoziierten Titel *La Comédie de la mort* könnte Liszt dem 1838 erschienenen Gedichtband von Théophile Gautier entnommen haben. Mit dem satirischen Titel des Bandes zielte er wohl auf die geistesverwandte Holzschnittreihe *Todtentanz* von Hans Holbein dem Jüngeren (1497–1543), die er vielleicht im Juni 1835 in Basel besichtigt hatte. Der andere von Liszt notierte Werktitel *Le Triomphe de la mort* verweist auf das seinerzeit Orcagna (um 1310–1368), heute aber Buonamico Buffalmacco (1. Hälfte des 14. Jh.) zugeschriebene Fresko auf dem Camposanto in Pisa, das Liszt Anfang 1839 aufgesucht hatte. Die dann im Tagebuch eingetragenen Pläne zu zwei Kompositionen sollten hinterher vermutlich eins werden und realisierten sich letztlich im *Totentanz*, als dessen Inspirator Liszt um 1850 Holbein, nach 1860 Orcagna nannte.

Die Kompositionsarbeit begann im Herbst 1847. Bis zum 28. November beendete Liszt die Hälfte des Werks, das er in einem zu diesem Zeitpunkt verfassten Brief (und zumeist

---

[1] R 134, SW/SH 470, NG2 A16a; NLA II/16.
[2] Zu den Quellen und zur Entstehungsgeschichte siehe K-LLT.
[3] Die vorliegende „Dies irae"-Bearbeitung ließ Liszt in sein in der 2. Hälfte der 1850er Jahre verwendete, sogenannte „Tasso"-Skizzenbuch (D-WRgs *60 / N5*, S. 115) eintragen. Siehe das Faksimile auf Seite 10. Vgl. MLTS, S. 373.
[4] Md'A-M, Bd. II, S. 219.

auch in weiteren) *Danse des morts* bezeichnete.[5] Die Inspirationsquelle machte er über den Titel hinaus durch die Nennung Holbeins eindeutig und erklärte dies ebenso in einem auf den 30. Dezember 1849 datierten Brief.[6] Da ungefähr zu dieser Zeit in einem Skizzenbuch-Eintrag auch der Titel „Campo Santo de Pisa – (Danse des Morts)" erscheint,[7] ist davon auszugehen, dass dann schon die beiden Kompositionspläne von 1839 miteinander verschmolzen waren. Der Skizzenbuch-Eintrag liefert auch unter dem Gesichtspunkt der Besetzung wertvolle Information. Während nämlich der Brief von 1847 über die Besetzung schweigt, definiert derjenige von 1849 jedoch die Komposition als eine für Klavier und Orchester geschriebene Fantasie, bis dahin führt das Skizzenbuch den *Totentanz* im Inhaltsverzeichnis des um 1850 zusammengestellten *Italia*-Bandes der *Années de pèlerinage* auf.[8] Obwohl sich der Inhalt des Bandes bald änderte, verrät die Einordnung des *Totentanz*es, dass der Plan einer Fassung des Werkes zu zwei Händen bereits in dieser Zeit aufgetaucht war.

Die aus den 1840/50er-Jahren erhalten gebliebenen musikalischen Quellen bewahrten ausnahmslos die Materialien der Klavier–Orchester-Version. Außer der „Dies irae"-Sequenz enthält jeder der Entwürfe eine Bearbeitung des 129. (130.) Psalms für vier Stimmen, die 1834–35 als musikalischer Ausgangspunkt des für Klavier und Orchester komponierten *De profundis* diente,[9] und die im 1853 veröffentlichten *Pensée des morts* ihren endgültigen Platz erlangte.[10] Vermutlich sich die Einheit der Komposition vor Augen haltend, entfernte Liszt etwa 1859 oder 1861[11] den Psalm aus dem *Totentanz* und gestaltete die endgültige Fassung der Komposition aus. Im Wissen um die Neuartigkeit des Werkes zö-

gerte er jedoch noch Jahre lang mit dessen Veröffentlichung. Am 12. November 1864 bat er Hans von Bülow um Rat,[12] der als Antwort mit dem Verleger Siegel in Leipzig zu verhandeln begann. Nachdem sie sich geeinigt hatten, betraute Liszt am 26. November Bülow mit den Obliegenheiten der Veröffentlichung,[13] bald darauf machte er sich an die Ausarbeitung der Klavierversion zu zwei Händen.[14] Er schrieb nur die Abschnitte nieder, die in der Version zu zwei Händen von den Solopartien der Klavier–Orchester-Version abweichen.[15] Außer diesem siebenseitigen Autograph standen der vorliegenden Ausgabe als Quellen noch die Klavierstimme der Erstausgabe der Klavier–Orchester-Version[16] sowie die von Liszt korrigierte Klavierstimme der Kopie, auf der die Erstausgabe basiert, zur Verfügung.[17] Als ergänzende Quellen wurden die der endgültigen vorhergehende Fassung der Klavier–Orchester-Version, im Detail die von Liszt korrigierte Klavierstimme der Partiturabschrift[18] sowie das zusätzliche autographe Material von letzterem berücksichtigt.[19]

Die für Klavier sowie für Klavier und Orchester komponierten Versionen des *Totentanz*es, ferner die Bearbeitung für zwei Klaviere erschienen 1865 im Druck.[20] Die Widmung des Werkes richtet sich an Bülow, der Solist bei der Uraufführung der Klavier–Orchester-Version war. Bei der misslungenen Aufführung am 15. April 1865 in Den Haag dirigierte Jean Verhulst.[21] Den *Totentanz* brachte erst Nikolai Rubinstein in seinen Konzerten in Sankt Petersburg, Moskau und Warschau im Jahre 1867 zum Erfolg.[22] Das Datum der Uraufführung der Version zu zwei Händen ist nicht bekannt.

Adrienne Kaczmarczyk
(Übersetzung von Anne Vester)

[5] „La Danse des Morts de Holbein est à moitié écrite, mais si [vous] ne voulez pas occasioner une malade mortelle qui pourrait s'opposer à son achèvement, tranquillisez-moi au plus tôt sur le sort de ma malles." Brief Liszts an M. Huber. Sotheby's Auktionskatalog, 15. Mai 1996, Nr. 397.

[6] „Was die Klaviermusik betrifft, so beendete ich unter anderem zwei sinfonische Konzerte und eine Fantasie mit Orchesterbegleitung, deren Hauptgedanken ich aus Holbeins Totentanz entnahm." Liszts an Julius Benedict verfasster Brief, in ELL, S. 126. Das Original des Briefes stand uns nicht zur Verfügung.

[7] „Ce qu'on entend" Skizzenbuch (D-WRgs *60 / N1*), S. 30.

[8] Die Zusammenstellung ist veröffentlicht in: NLA S/13, S. XXII, XLV.

[9] R 668, SW/SH 691, NG2 H3.

[10] R 14, SW/SH 173, NG2 A158; NLA I/9; Frühfassung: SH 172a, NG2 A61; NLA S/6.

[11] Lina Ramann legt die Ausarbeitung der endgültigen Fassung auf 1859 fest, Richard Pohl auf 1861, aber sie begründen ihre Datierungen nicht. Vgl. RLKM II/2, S. 345 bzw. PFL, S. 228.

[12] BL-B, S. 323.

[13] BL-B, S. 324–325.

[14] „Quant à la Danse macabre je crois que pour plus de clarté, il y a lieu d'allonger le titre avec les vocables de // »Paraphrase de la Danse des Morts. Dies irae.« // Je vous ai dit dernièrement que j'avais écrit à Siegel en réponse à sa demande de faire une seconde édition de la Danse macabre pour piano seul. J'écrirai volontiers les quelques pages de notes nécessaires à cet effet quand il m'aura fait parvenir la partition, et en les lui envoyant, j'ajouterai la dédicace qui devra être placée sur une autre page à part. Vous êtes trop un homme à part pour que votre nom soit entremêlé au titre." Liszts Brief an Bülow vom 9. Dezember 1864. In BL-B, S. 326.

[15] Eigentümerin des Autographs ist die Washingtoner The Library of Congress. Signatur: *M196. L58*.

[16] Plattennummer: 2814; Exemplar: H-Bl *Z 3802*.

[17] D-WRgs *60 / H 10*.

[18] US-NYpm, The Robert Lehman Collection, *115178*.

[19] Eigentümerin ist Ester Bonacossa, Marchesa della Valle di Casanova (Milano).

[20] Plattennummer der Fassung zu zwei Händen: 2815. HM: September–Oktober, 1865, S. 159. Exemplar: H-Bl *LGy 509*.

[21] BL-B, S. 329.

[22] Siehe Liszts Brief vom 5. Dezember 1883 an Carolyne von Sayn-Wittgenstein: Br. 7, S. 393.

ABOUT THE EDITION

Publication of Ferenc Liszt's (1811–1886) musical works, writings and correspondence and the compilation of a thematic catalogue of his creative oeuvre began in the 20th century and is still in progress. The work of producing a complete edition of his musical œuvre was launched in 1907 by the Franz Liszt Stiftung established by Grand Duke Carl Alexander Saxe-Weimar-Eisenach and supported by Princess Marie von Hohenlohe. This so-called old Complete Edition, 33 volumes of which were completed by 1936, contains a third of Liszt's life-work. In 1970, with the aim of modernizing and completing this old edition, Editio Musica Budapest (EMB) launched a new, scholarly critical edition of the musical works.

The New Liszt Edition (NLE) comprises ten series, the works being grouped according to genre and scoring. Series I (Works for piano solo) was completed as a joint publication of EMB and Bärenreiter-Verlag, Kassel, by 1985. From 1986 on, EMB continued to publish NLE alone, completing Series II (Free arrangements and transcriptions for piano solo) by 2005. In publishing Series I and II priority was given to the definitive version of the works; of early versions only those were published in the appendix that differed significantly from the definitive form. In 2005 a series of 15 supplementary volumes was launched with the aim of publishing early versions of the solo piano works that differ less substantially from the definitive form: mainly those published by Liszt himself, but also some that remained in manuscript. In special cases more extensive fragments are also published in the supplementary volumes.

The separate editions of Liszt's solo piano works already published in NLE provide not only authentic texts based on scholarly research and critical notes but also complete early versions, as well as prefaces containing important background information.

*

In editing an attempt has been made to adhere to Liszt's compositional and notational peculiarities to the greatest extent possible. Thus the sections notated in an unusual, simplifying manner are not changed to agree with the rules of present-day notation if this makes the appearance of the score too crammed. The rhythm is not made regular in places where the time of striking a note is defined exclusively by the horizontal division. On the other hand, the inconsistencies within the simplifications are eliminated in every case. The so-called orchestral manner of notation is retained throughout: the stems are not drawn in the customary direction in these places. Rest signs for two or more parts in the same hand are only added if their absence would have made the timing, the place in the rhythm for sounding the subsequent note, uncertain. The size of the note heads – normal (big), smaller and very small – follows the sources exactly. Appoggiaturas of different value consisting of one note are written uniformly as quavers with a stroke through their stem and their slurs have been tacitly added. The value of very small notes is corrected only if they form an integral part of the rhythm. Fermatas substituted for additional value and placed above blank staves are left as they are, no rest sign being added under them. In chromatic passages the same accidentals are repeatedly written out within one and the same bar to improve legibility. In the case of *quasi cadenza, a capriccio, a piacere* and *rubato* directions the values are not modified, nor are any changes of time indicated separately. Sections marked *ossia* and written for pianos with a range of less than seven octaves are included in the 'Critical Notes' since their relevance for present-day practice is insignificant. The original slurring shown in the sources has been retained; even slurs referring simultaneously to two parts are left unchanged. Where the sources do not prescribe the use of the pedal no pedalling is suggested since the lack of pedal signs does not necessarily mean *senza pedale:* the *armonioso* style of playing, for example explicitly requires frequent use of the pedal. In cancelling *una corda* the requirements both of dynamics and of the change of timbre have been considered. The indication *due pedali (mettez les deux pédales)* in the sources is replaced by *con ped., una corda* in the present edition, the change of instruction being mentioned in the 'Critical Notes' in each case. The > signs occurring midway between two staves are written out in both hands. The broken line after *riten., accel.,* and other tempo indications marks the duration of validity of the given direction; consequently, *a tempo* is not added at the end of the lines. In the pieces Liszt's original fingering is given everywhere. Fingering is added in identical musical sections only if the sources indicate the fingering at a later place or places. Liszt's peculiar performance signs, which are no longer used today, have been retained. Of these the large Λ and > (accent) as well as the ⌒ (pause) signs affect the whole group of notes joined by them. The meaning of the other signs is explained in the footnotes on each occasion. *NB* always marks an original footnote or instruction; the footnotes supplied with an asterisk stem from the editors. In exceptional instances even a footnote with an asterisk may derive from the original. In this case, however, it is distinguished by the remark 'original footnote'.

Editorial additions are differentiated from the original as follows:

Letters (words, dynamics and trill signs) by italics;

Triplet etc. figures by small-sized numbers printed in italics;

Accidentals, staccato dots and wedges, pedal signs and asterisks, rest signs, tenuto and accent signs, fermatas and ornaments by smaller type;

Crescendo and diminuendo signs, round brackets, the wavy lines of trills, large-sized accent signs and fermatas by fainter lines;

Time signatures by fainter numbers between the staves;

Slurs by dotted lines.

All other additions appear between square brackets.

In order to meet the practical requirements of the NLE and to help solving the performing difficulties of the works involved, the editors have also included Liszt's verbal directions for performance put down by August Göllerich in his diary after his piano classes with Liszt as well as those preserved in Lina Ramann's *Liszt-Pädagogium* and in other reliable sources.

To facilitate identification of the works, their number in Raabe's, Searle–Winklhofer's, Eckhardt–Mueller's and Short–Howard's catalogues has also been added.

PREFACE

TOTENTANZ – DANSE MACABRE
Paraphrase über 'Dies irae'
R 188, SW/SH 525, NG2 A62

Totentanz / Danse macabre [Dance of Death] belongs among the major achievements of Liszt's Weimar years, even though the genesis of its composition crosses the borders of this period in both directions. Its inspirational background consists of musical and artistic experiences Liszt underwent in the 1830s, though the work was published as late as 1865, after the composer had moved to Rome.

Liszt had probably been contemplating basing a work on the 'Dies irae' melody since December 1830, the Paris premiere of Berlioz's *Symphonie fantastique*. The symphony's elaborate piano score which he finished in 1833 testifies to his early interest,[1] as does the fact that the *Dance of Death* makes use of a French arrangement of the sequence in alternatim fashion.[2] In this version the odd strophes are sung to the original melody attributed to Thomas of Celano, while the even ones have more recent four-part music that also appears in Liszt's version in strophe 6 (bar 466).[3]

A concrete plan to compose the work can first be traced to a diary entry of February 1839. Liszt mentioned the titles of two works without defining their genre or instrumentation, one being connected with the name of Holbein, the other with that of Orcagna.[4] Liszt may have borrowed the title *La Comédie de la mort*, which he associated with the German painter, from the title page of Théophile Gautier's 1838 collection of poems. The title of this satirical volume was arguably meant as a reference to Hans Holbein the Younger's (1497–1543) kindred set of engravings entitled *Todtentanz*, which Liszt may have seen in June 1835 in Basel. The other

title jotted down by Liszt, *Le Triomphe de la mort*, refers to a fresco in the Campo Santo at Pisa, then attributed to Orcagna (*c*1310–1368) and today to Buonamico Buffalmacco (1st half of the 14th century), which Liszt visited in early 1839. At a later stage the plans of the two compositions registered in the diary were probably merged and eventually materialized in the *Dance of Death*, which Liszt around 1850 said was inspired by Holbein, and after 1860 said was inspired by Orcagna.

Liszt began work in the autumn of 1847. By 28 November he had completed half of the composition which he called *Danse des morts* in one of his letters from the period (and mostly in later ones as well).[5] Apart from the title, he also clarified the source of inspiration by naming Holbein, and made a similar statement in a letter dated 30 December 1849.[6] Given that a sketchbook entry from the same period also includes the title 'Campo Santo de Pisa – (Danse des Morts)',[7] then by this time the two 1839 plans were likely merged. The note in the sketchbook also provides an important clue regarding its instrumentation. Whereas the 1847 letter remains silent on this matter, and the one from 1849 defines the composition as a fantasia written for piano and orchestra, in the sketchbook *Dance of Death* appears in the table of contents of the *Italian* volume of *Années de pèlerinage* that took shape around 1850.[8] Even though the contents of this volume were soon changed, the inclusion of *Dance of Death* reveals that the idea of a version for two hands emerged already at this time.

---

[1] R 134, SW/SH 470, NG2 A16a; NLE II/16.

[2] On the sources and the genesis of the work, see K-LLT.

[3] Liszt had this 'Dies irae' arrangement copied into the 'Tasso' sketchbook he used in the second half of the 1850s (D-WRgs *60 / N5*, p. 115). See the facsimile on page 10. Cf. MLTS, p. 373.

[4] Md'A-M, vol. 2, p. 219.

[5] 'La Danse des Morts de Holbein est à moitié écrite, mais si [vous] ne voulez pas occasioner une malade mortelle qui pourrait s'opposer à son achèvement, tranquillisez-moi au plus tôt sur le sort de ma malles.' Liszt's letter to M. Huber. Sotheby's auction catalogue, 15 May 1996, no. 397.

[6] 'As for piano music, among others I have completed two symphonic concertos and a fantasia with orchestral accompaniment, the main idea of which I have taken from Holbein's Dance of Death.' Liszt's letter to Julius Benedict, in ELL, p. 126. We were not able to consult the original of this letter.

[7] 'Ce qu'on entend' sketchbook (D-WRgs *60 / N1*), p. 30.

[8] The list is reproduced in NLE S/13, pp. XXII, XLV.

The sources dating from the 1840s and 1850s invariably preserve materials for the version for piano and orchestra. Apart from the 'Dies irae' sequence, each of the drafts contains a four-part arrangement of Psalm No. 129 (130) which served as the starting point for the *De profundis* for piano and orchestra in 1834–35,[9] and found its final place in *Pensée des morts* in 1853.[10] Perhaps in 1859 or 1861,[11] presumably in order to preserve the unity of the composition, Liszt omitted the psalm from the *Dance of Death*, and created the definitive version. Being keenly aware of the innovative features of the work he hesitated for years whether or not to publish it. On 12 November 1864 he asked for Hans von Bülow's advice,[12] who in response began negotiations with the publisher Siegel in Leipzig. Once they had come to an agreement, on 26 November Liszt entrusted the preparations of the edition to Bülow,[13] and set to work on the version for two hands.[14] He notated only those passages of the latter version that differ from the solo part of the version for piano and orchestra.[15] Apart from this seven-page autograph the present edition relies on the solo part of the first edition of the version for piano and orchestra[16] and the piano part of a copy corrected by Liszt that served as its basis.[17] As a supplementary source we have consulted the pre-definitive form of the version for piano and orchestra, specifically the piano part of the copy corrected by the composer,[18] and the autograph material that complements it.[19]

The versions for piano as well as for piano and orchestra were published in 1865, as was the transcription for two pianos.[20] The *Dance of Death* was dedicated to Bülow, who played the solo part at the premiere of the version for piano and orchestra. This unsuccessful performance on 15 April 1865 in The Hague was conducted by Jean Verhulst.[21] The first pianist to have success with the *Dance of Death* was Nikolai Rubinstein in his 1867 concerts in Saint Petersburg, Moscow and Warsaw.[22] The date of the first performance of the version for two hands is unknown.

Adrienne Kaczmarczyk
(translated by Balázs Mikusi)

[9] R 668, SW/SH 691, NG2 H3.

[10] R 14, SW/SH 173, NG2 A158; NLE I/9; early version: SH 172a, NG2 A61; NLE S/6.

[11] Lina Ramann dates the definitive version to 1859, Richard Pohl to 1861, but neither provides justification for the respective hypotheses. Cf. RLKM II/2, p. 345, and PFL, p. 228.

[12] BL-B, p. 323.

[13] BL-B, pp. 324–325.

[14] 'Quant à la Danse macabre je crois que pour plus de clarté, il y a lieu d'allonger le titre avec les vocables de // "Paraphrase de la Danse des Morts. Dies irae." // Je vous ai dit dernièrement que j'avais écrit à Siegel en réponse à sa demande de faire une seconde édition de la Danse macabre pour piano seul. J'écrirai volontiers les quelques pages de notes nécessaires à cet effet quand il m'aura fait parvenir la partition, et en les lui envoyant, j'ajouterai la dédicace qui devra être placée sur une autre page à part. Vous êtes trop un homme à part pour que votre nom soit entremêlé au titre.' Liszt's letter to Bülow dated 9 December 1864. In BL-B, p. 326.

[15] The autograph is owned by The Library of Congress in Washington DC. Shelfmark: *ML96 .L58, Case.*

[16] Plate number: 2814; copy: H-Bl *Z 3802.*

[17] D-WRgs *60 / H 10.*

[18] US-NYpm, The Robert Lehman Collection, *115178.*

[19] The owner of the autograph is Ester Bonacossa, Marchesa della Valle di Casanova (Milan).

[20] Plate number of the version for two hands: 2815. HM: September–October 1865 (p. 159). Copy: H-Bl *LGy 509.*

[21] BL-B, p. 329.

[22] See Liszt's 5 December 1883 letter to Carolyne von Sayn-Wittgenstein: Br. 7, p. 393.

10

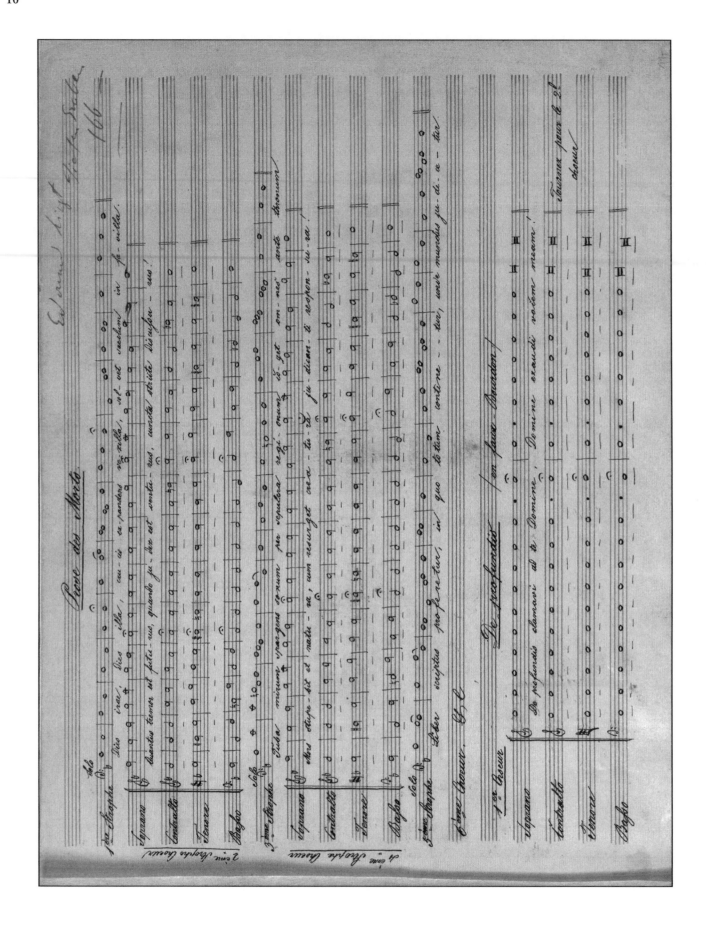

Prose des Morts: die dem *Totentanz / Danse macabre* zugrunde liegende „Dies irae"-Bearbeitung. Nicht identifizierte Handschrift in Liszts „Tasso"-Skizzenbuch (f. 74r, S. 147).

Prose des Morts: the 'Dies irae' arrangement that served as basis for *Totentanz / Danse macabre*. Written in an unidentified hand in Liszt's 'Tasso' sketchbook (f. 74r, p. 147).

Klassik Stiftung Weimar, Goethe- und Schiller-Archiv. Signatur / Shelfmark: *60 / N5*.

Foto / Photo: Klassik Stiftung Weimar

Hans von Bülow gewidmet

TOTENTANZ – DANSE MACABRE

Paraphrase über „Dies irae"

R 188, SW/SH 525, NG2 A62

FRANZ LISZT

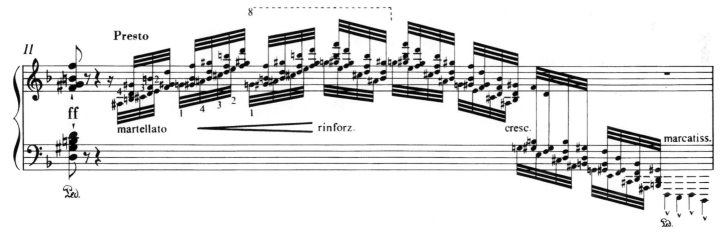

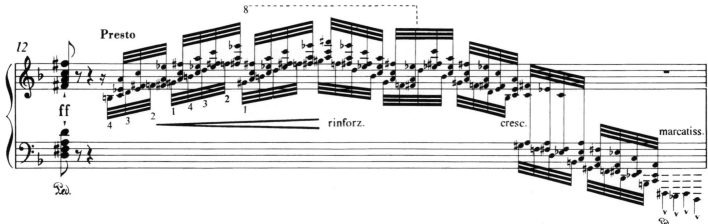

Z. 12 718

13

Z. 12718

14

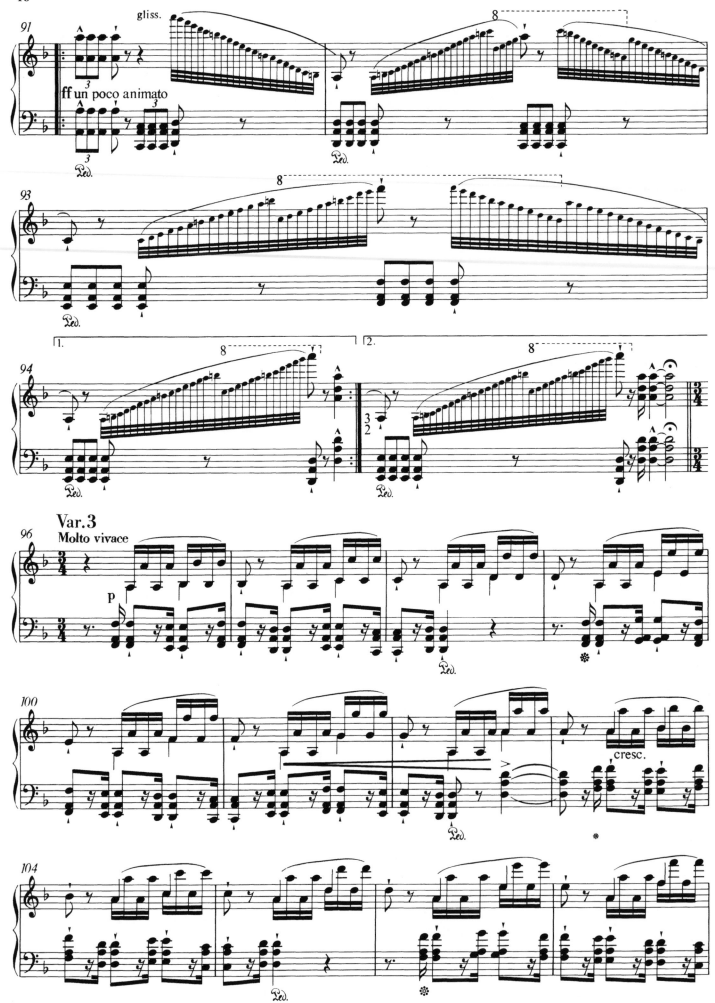

Var. 4 (canonique)

Cadenza ad libitum

entweder gleich weiter
zum Fugato (Seite 20),   oder

either go directly
to the Fugato (page 20),   or

Zur Kürzung weiter Fugato (Seite 20)
For abridging go to the Fugato (page 20)

Var. 5 (Fugato)

*) Das lange marcato-Zeichen der rechten Hand bezieht sich auf alle drei Töne. (Ebenso in Takten 241, 245 und 249.)

The long marcato sign in the right hand refers to all three notes. (Similarly in bars 241, 245 and 249.)

Z. 12718

Zur Kürzung weiter Cadenza (Seite 32)
For abridging go to the Cadenza (page 32)

Zur Kürzung weiter Seite 32, Fortsetzung der Cadenza, Zeichen ⊕
For abridging go to the page 32, continuation of the Cadenza, sign ⊕

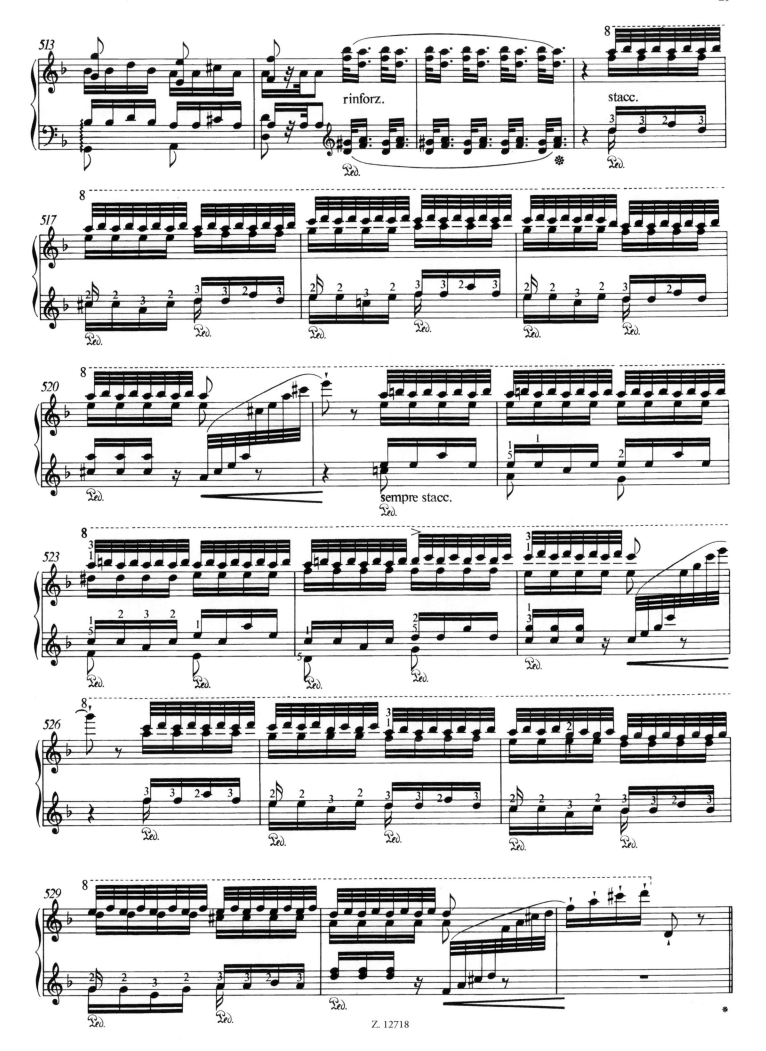

CRITICAL NOTES

TOTENTANZ – DANSE MACABRE

Sources

A: the first edition, published in 1865: 'Hans von Bülow / gewidmet. / TODTENTANZ. / (Danse macabre.) / PARAPHRASE / über / "DIES IRAE" / für / Piano und Orchester / von / FR. LISZT. / ... / Arrangement für Pianoforte allein ... / LEIPZIG, C. F. SIEGEL.' Plate No. 2815.

B: the autograph manuscript (US-Wc *ML96, .L58, Case*). The manuscript consists of seven pages of music paper (upright format) with thirty-two staves per page and letters (*a–g*) instead of page numbers. The title on page *a*, above the first line of music, is '*Todten Tanz' für Pianoforte allein*. In the music there are many abbreviations as Liszt did not fully write out the bars which are the same in the piano part of the version for orchestra and piano; he marked these bars to be taken from that version by using the page numbers of the first edition of the score (see 'C'). The bars in question are: **11**, **12** and **15** except for the first quaver, and then **41–50, 59–66, 71–82, 124–157, 167–218, 251–270, 305–311, 319–324, 341–350, 393–465, 532–583**, and **590–600**. **83–90** and **91–95** were also to be used in part. For these bars the piano part in the first edition of the orchestral score has been used as the chief source for this present edition.

C: the bars of the piano part as listed in 'B' from the first edition of the score of the original version for piano and orchestra. (Siegel, Leipzig. Plate No. 2814. A copy from the Liszt estate, now in H-Bl, shelfmark *Z 3802*.)

D: the bars of the piano part as listed in 'B' from a copy, corrected by Liszt himself, of the piano and orchestra version (D-WRgs *60 / H 10*).

Supplementary Sources

E: the bars of the piano part as listed in 'B' and agreeing with 'C' in an autograph manuscript of the score of the piano and orchestra version belonging to Ester Bonacossa, Marchesa della Valle di Casanova, Milan.

F: the bars of the piano part as listed in 'B' and agreeing with 'C' in a copy, corrected by Liszt himself, of the score of the piano and orchestra version. (US-NYpm, The Robert O. Lehmann Collection, *115178*.)

It is to be noted that neither 'E' nor 'F' are in themselves complete: supplementing each other, these two sources contain an earlier version of the work which is not the same as the final version.

In distinguishing between staccato dots and staccatissimo dashes the autograph manuscripts (and Liszt's own corrections in 'D' and 'F') have been given great importance. In this context the supplementary sources have also been used as main sources and changes made on the basis of the supplementary sources have not been listed in the Critical Notes.

11, 12: at the end of the bar there is a fermata sign above the right hand rest in 'A' and 'C'. Since there is nothing to justify writing this sign in the right hand only, in **12** 'F' has been followed, and in **11** the fermata has correspondingly been omitted.

15: in the main sources there is a very short crescendo and diminuendo sign under each of the first two notes in the 16th triplet of the Cadenza. This is a misprint arising from a misreading by the engraver and here it has been corrected to agree with 'E'.

In front of the 2nd octave in the right hand of the third semiquaver group from the end of the Cadenza, the naturals have been added.

20: the sharp has been added before the 5th note in the right hand.

41–45: in the principal sources the right hand slur goes on to the 2nd minim in **43**. This slur has been corrected to agree with 'E'.

54: in 'A' there is a staccato dot in the left hand. In accordance with the three preceding bars, this has been changed to a staccatissimo sign.

59: the staccato dots on the 4th and 6th notes in the right hand have been added by analogy with **51**.

67, 71: the staccato dots for the lower voice on the 3rd and 4th crotchets in the right hand have been added.

68, 70: the slur beginning at the minim has been added in both hands to agree with **72** and **74**.

75, 82: in 'A' and 'C' the right hand slurs are extended to the last quaver of the bar. In the present edition the slurring in 'F' has been followed.

78: in 'F' and 'D' the last two semiquavers in the right hand are a^1-b $flat^1$. In spite of this, 'A' and 'C' have been followed here (in 'B' this bar is not written out) as Liszt might have changed these two notes in the engraver's manuscript or on the proofsheets of the score (their whereabouts are unknown).

80, 81: in the main sources there is a staccato dot on the last note in the right hand. This has been corrected to a staccatissimo sign to agree with the analogous parts of **75–79** and **82** and with 'D'.

81: the *e* in the 1st chord in the right hand has been added to agree with 'F'.

82: in the main sources the 2nd slur in the left hand extends to the last note. In accordance with the right hand slur and in order to agree with **78**, the slur is not extended to the last note in this edition.

The staccato dot in the left hand has been added to agree with the right hand.

85: in the sources the 1st staccato dot in the right hand is not included.

86: the staccato dot on the 3rd note in the left hand has been corrected to a staccatissimo sign to agree with the preceding bars.

86, 88, 89: the staccato dot in the right hand has been corrected to a staccatissimo sign to agree with the preceding bars.

90: in 'A' there is a staccato dot on the 6th note in the left hand. This has been altered to a staccatissimo sign by analogy with **89** and **90**.

92–95: in 'A' there are staccato dots in the right hand. They have been altered to staccatissimo signs here to agree with **83–89**.

95: the sources do not include the staccatissimo sign in the left hand.

103: the star marking the release of the pedal has been added since no pedal is prescribed in the analogous **96**.

109: the staccatissimo sign at the 3rd chord in the left hand has been added – or, rather, the staccato dot in 'C' has been corrected to a staccatissimo sign – by analogy with **102**.

110: the sources do not include the 1st staccatissimo sign in the right hand.

117: the sources do not include the staccatissimo sign in the left hand.

121: in 'A' there is a staccato dot at the 2nd chord in the right hand. This has been corrected to a staccatissimo sign to agree with the left hand.

132: in the main sources the 2nd slur in the right hand starts from the 4th note of the top part. To agree with the analogous part of **130** and **131**, the slur has here been started from the top note of the arpeggio chord.

167–171: 'A' and 'C' have staccato dots everywhere. These have been corrected to staccatissimo signs in accordance with the *sempre staccato molto* prescribed in **171** and with 'D'. This alteration at the 1st note in **167** is also justified by the analogy with the **175**.

190: only 'E' has the accent.

194: in the main sources the slur extends to the 1st note of the next bar. This has been corrected to agree with 'E'.

198: in 'A' and 'C' there is a staccato dot on the 3rd note. This has been altered to a staccatissimo sign to agree with the preceding bars.

212: in 'E' and 'D' there is a flat before the 2nd note in the left hand and the 1st note in the right hand of **213**. Here 'A' and 'C' have been followed since Liszt might have corrected these two signs the way it is mentioned at **78** in the Critical Notes.

226: the star marking the release of the pedal has been added because in the analogous section beginning at **219** no pedal is prescribed.

229, 318: the staccato dot in the left hand has been changed to a staccatissimo sign to agree with the right hand.

301, 303, 305, 312: the staccato dots in the right and left hands have been changed to staccatissimo signs by analogy with **314, 316** and **318**.

304: in the sources the 3rd staccatissimo sign in the left hand is missing.

317: the *Ped.* marking has been added by analogy with **304**.

350: the star marking the release of the pedal has been added to agree with the identical **354**.

356: the left hand accent has been added to agree with the right hand.

381: in the sources there is no left hand slur.

393: the *ff* occured originally in bar **397** and only in 'A'.

408: the star marking the release of the pedal has been added by analogy with **396, 400** and **404**.

424: in the left hand in the second half of the 'D' has been followed by analogy with **431**. 'A' and 'C' repeat here exactly the notes of **422**, while 'B' here merely refers to 'C'.

505–506; 510–511: the staccatissimo signs have been added by analogy with **500–501**.

544: there is no *Ped.* in the sources.

547: in 'A' there is the marking *Ped.* under the 1st note in the left hand. This is clearly a misprint. Here it is replaced by a star since no pedal is prescribed in the similar section in **553–557** and **559–563**.

563: the natural in front of the last note in the left hand has been added.

565: the star marking the release of the pedal has been added by analogy with **553** and **559**.

569: the staccatissimo signs have been added here, instead of the staccato dots in 'A', by analogy with **575** and **582**.

589: in 'A' there is also a *b flat[1]* in the 1st chord of the right hand. This is clearly a misprint and has been corrected to agree with the identical part in the left hand.

590: the natural in front of the *f* in the 14th chord in the right hand has been added.

The natural in front of the 6th chord in the left hand has been added.

In the 5th bar of the Cadenza, marked by dotted bar lines, the 3rd beam of the demisemiquavers has been added because in performance the rhythm of the thematic material should be precise.

The last *Ped.* marking has been added to agree with the third one preceding it.

Imre Sulyok, Imre Mező
(translated by Fred Macnicol)

Felelős kiadó az Editio Musica Budapest Zeneműkiadó Kft. igazgatója
Z. 12 718/10 (6,3 A/5 ív); 2022
Felelős szerkesztő: Mező Imre, Mikusi Eszter
Műszaki szerkesztő: Tihanyi Éva
A sorozatcímlapot Fodor Attila tervezte

Ptinted in Hungary